I0559383

I'll Find My Way

By Reggie Baity

DAYDREAM

Saw grass gently blows as the colorful sky glows
Sounds of water and smell of salt,
refreshes my mind as I walk
Cool breezes along the shore,
types of nights loved ones adore
Floating above, watching the nightfall,
enjoying the weather, just loving it all
At ease in a world of my own, no negativity,
the dead thoughts are gone
My mind is clear and alive, the night is filled as I vibe
Loud noises brings me back,
back to reality just like that
People yelling, I hear the scream,
take me back, take me back, but it was all a dream...

2

PAIN IS REAL

Emotions are drastically wild,
suicidal thoughts are foul
Running from the pain, realizing there is no gain
Sickness, do not play, it will eat you up day by day
Dad is a cancer patient,
being strong becoming impatient
Mom has working memory, lost soul,
don't know who's the enemy
This pain I feel, hazardous and it is real

4

YEARS OF TEARS

Feeling all down, face full of tears,
Feeling this pain for the past few years
Feeling sick to my stomach, nauseating vomit
No moe' real friends fake friends plummet
Angered by other souls' head held low
Feelings, no goals, I think I'm about to blow.

6

ALONE

Painful emotions thick like smoke clouds,
Killing me slowly while smiling through crowds,
Black evil thoughts decaying my brain,
poisonous effect leaving a major stain,
Surrounded by many people but feeling alone,
my brain is dead and feel like it is gone,
Steady drifting away from people,
thoughts getting crazy becoming lethal,
No one to help me with this pain,
no reset button this is not a game,
The headaches grew into migraines,
the pain I'm feeling is insane,
After crying and shaking I drop to my knees,
looking up help me father please,
Everyday I began to pray, as my life change I began to
feel okay, Life is hard never back down,
accept the task and wear the crown.

MY HEART

I remember when you first met me, you didn't believe,
stereotyped me because you couldn't see,
I stepped up and showed you now you agree,
changed your mindset by just being me,
I love you, baby you are mine; no love is perfect,

UNIQUE

Pretty and gorgeous, one of a kind...
true to self with a strong mind.
Talking to you smiling all day,
enjoying your time, I must say
Erasing my pain, killing my scars...
very sweet like candy bars
Time flies everything feels right.
dancing and singing under the moonlight
Night ends as the nightfall,
kissing you, giving you my all
Time to say goodnight...
smooches yea that's about right

PATIENCE

All my life, I wanted someone good,
Patience was a virtue I never really understood
Mishaps and letdowns, grievance with ripped gowns
Years go by feeling lonely,
just wanting that one and only
Then you, I mean just you,
wondering could this be is this true
Headstrong ambition built like a queen,
passionate loving is this my dream
So attractive but bigger than that, with you,
I know you have my back
Walk hand in hand together,
grow old and old with rose petals forever
Live life like queen and king,
I believe this is my dream
All I wanted was someone good,
now I see patience is really understood

COMPLETE

Two hearts, one beat, our love equals concrete,
I got you; you got me
And your heart where I stand,
promise to be there till the end

START TO FINISH

The dark sky flows, the wind steady blows
Time won't stop, fake images on top
People talking, Grieving about the past, fighting,
knowing this is not the last
Pushing for me but really despise me,
I will be what I set out to be,
your negativity fuel, shining like a hand full of jewels
Starting point just my beginning,
my potential so strong it's never ending
No matter what I go through, I will bounce back head-
strong I won't lose focus of my track
People hate to see you succeed,
never want you to take lead,
Society is all types of corrupt,
I'm at the bottom I promise I'm going up
Nothing can stop me I am me
Living legend just watch and see

PHANTOM

People drive you away, hidden smiles keep you safe
Frontin' to be this, when reality you aren't it
Hatin' on others to stand above,
in reality at the bottom getting no love
So confused and lost, brain trapped in paying the cost
Ghostly soul, dark and lethal,
bullet words just as equal
Vision of two which one to choose,
I have to focus quick before I lose
Disease from being two face,
killing others, I need to stay in place
Encourage your peers to be great before
something happens, and it's too late
Love one another as you will learn to love others

20

TWO DOVES

My friend, my heart, my love,
you made me whole made me feel above
I run, I jump, I swing; you make
me happy with all the small things
One day, life suddenly change,
dreams shattered, feeling strange
Impulsive movements cannot think,
panicking, heavy breathing, no time to blink
How could you why to me,
I love you I had faith how could this be
You played with another soul,
not caring about the load or the toll
The abandonment of crushed heart
left me dying in rage, falling apart
The ultimate crush has hit me, my love has failed... you
were with someone who's not me
Trust is gone the ultimate betrayal dissed me
should I retaliate and hang your ass on a rail
My friend, my heart, my love,
how could you kill this dove

22

NO DEFEAT, I BELIEVE

No defeat, I believe
Growing up in a small city, nothing could be seen,
Eager to get it, ambition of a feign
Even when I want to quit, I know that's not for me
I hold my head high, I go in chase my dreams
There's no pressure, this my destiny
My pops showed me the way, he was my everything
The skies were so dark all I heard was the bark
Shattering my mind, had lost track of time
Couldn't stand on my feet, but I will not face defeat
Pops showed me the door,
I walked through on my own
How could I quit when I'm this strong
In myself, I believe it's like a sudden rush for me
When you believe, you will start to see
It's on you to succeed, I will succeed
No defeat, I believe

NO LIMITS

Life isn't fair, things happen, nobody cares
Hold on for a min listen to what I'm saying
Life isn't fair, things happen, nobody cares
How many of you been told you can't do it?
How many of you been told you aren't worth anything?
How many of you feel like you are alone?
How many of you get doubted daily?
How many of you feel you can't do it,
feel like everybody is against you?
How many of you want to quit and give up?
The real question is, who cares what they think?
Success has no limits, nobody cares if you are down.
Change your mindset, be positive, and know what you
want in life. Fight for your success like you would for
your last breath of air. Only you can limit your dream.
The people you are close to will try and derail your
dreams. People who do not have dreams are those of
dream killers. Remember, when you are feeling down,
and nobody is there for you, nobody has you like you
have you. Stop feeling sorry for yourself and change
your mindset. Life isn't fair be strong put yourself first.
Have courage, have dreams believe in self. Push for-
ward, dream big, chase your dreams change your mind-
set. Dream big there is no limit to success.

TUNNEL VISION

It's messed up, isn't it, how we see the world
Always complaining about every little thing, trying to
have a problem for no reason
It's messed up how selfish we are, never grateful for
what we have, letting our greed control what we see.
How many of us always complain about things we don't
have? Tunnel vision is harming your life. Open your eyes
and enjoy what you do have.
Now look at the people with real problems; I mean
real problems, people who were born with one leg, one
hand, a couple of fingers, blind.
What about people born with an illness who are fight-
ing for their life? What about the people who don't know
when they are going to eat? What about the people who
don't have a place to sleep at night
These people are the people with real vision, people
like us don't have real problems,
we have tunnel vision.
These people see life differently, they find a way to en-
joy the world through different aspects of life, they con-
tinue to fight every day, not complaining, a true symbol
of strength.
They enjoy what they have and life every day, not wast-
ing time complaining about what they don't have and
facing life's challenges.
So why complain about the simple, small stuff? Why
make problems for no reason? Why complain when
there is actually no real problem,
The vision the goal has to change, adversity is an ob-
stacle, we can change tunnel vision into vision, let's be
great no matter the obstacle in front of us.

27

NO EXCUSES

NO EXCUSES: Life is full of surprises, most people use the quote life isn't fair to justify their problems. Everybody has problems or situations that are tough for them. People make choices depending on self-knowledge or feelings at the time. How many of you can say you made a decision and never regretted it? How many of you can say you never said what if I did this better or did that better? How many of you can say you never judged someone because of how they look or what they are doing? Guess what? None of you can? The answer is simple to these questions; we are human; it's in our nature, but remember, everybody's situations and problems are different, everybody's feelings and hardships are different, and people handle things differently and react differently. Nobody can tell you how you feel about a situation and how it is affecting you. As people, we are our hardest self-critique. No more excuses, no more worrying about what your pupils think and feel. Remember, nobody got your back like you have your back. Things happen in our lives for a reason, that is, for experiences and learning. For those who do not learn, they go through the same hardships until the lesson is learned. How about us as people? Stop making excuses and go for it all. Stop letting people dictate your happiness. We are created equal we all can accomplish more. Speak

it in existence. Only you can get down on yourself and slow your dreams down. One thing, though, the clock doesn't stop ticking, time stops for no one. No excuse for what you do in life; don't use your past struggle or childhood or what your parents went through as an excuse. Excuses are not real; they are words and phrases for setbacks; every excuse weakens you mentally. How can you learn from mistakes if there is an excuse every time? You can't because you are always looking to get out of the situation and accept what you can't change and what you can't fix. Things turn out the best for those who make the best out of a situation. No more weak-minded people change your view, and it will change your life. Accept all flaws and mistakes, get barbarous and let's kill your excuses; wake up tomorrow with no excuses. Be stronger; your life will start to change; excuses are for the weak; I am no longer weak; I am strong, NO EXCUSES.

www.ingramcontent.com/pod-product-compliance
Lightning Source LLC
Chambersburg PA
CBHW051251120626
46547CB00014B/1902